Twelve Documents That Shaped the World

Mort Gerberg and Jerome Agel

A Perigee Book

Perigee Books
are published by
The Putnam Publishing Group
200 Madison Avenue
New York, NY 10016

Library of Congress Cataloging-in-Publication Data

Gerberg, Mort.
    Twelve documents that shaped the world / Mort Gerberg
and Jerome Agel.
        p. cm.
    "A Perigee book."
    ISBN 0-399-51746-4 (alk. paper)
    1. Civil rights—History—Sources.   2. Human rights—History
—Sources.   3. Liberty—History—Sources.   I. Agel, Jerome.
II. Title.
JC571.G43   1992   91-47064 CIP
323'.09—dc20

Book design by David Allen
Cover illustration © by Mort Gerberg

Printed in the United States of America
1 2 3 4 5 6 7 8 9 10

This book is printed on acid-free paper.

CONTENTS

(The twelve documents were selected by the publisher.)

Magna Carta

" . . . the men in our kingdom shall have . . . liberties, rights . . . "

June 15, 1215

Nearly eight centuries ago, in the Middle Ages, the most famous document in English constitutional history was reluctantly signed and sealed by King John "in the meadow which is called Runnymede between Windsor and Staines on the fifteenth day of June, in the seventeenth year of our reign."

It was late spring, 1215, and the document, written in medieval Latin script, was Magna Carta—Latin for "Great Charter." And a truly great charter it became, an enduring symbol in elegant and precise terms of limited government, the rule of law, and broadened civil rights. Magna Carta has inspired petitions of liberty throughout the world.

John was born in 1167, the youngest son of Henry II and the remarkable Eleanor of Aquitaine, and presently was nicknamed "Lackland" because he possessed no independent feudal estates of his own. He became king at the age of 32 on the death of his Crusading brother, Richard "Lion-Heart." A first-class administrator, John strove to run an efficient government. But his favorite tool was the royal prerogative, which, he claimed, permitted him to do anything he wanted to do. At times he was cruel and treacherous, provoking bitter opposition among his nobles, who felt that he ignored or abused the traditional feudal relationship between Crown and nobility. On his own authority, John levied heavy taxes and extorted money from the barons to finance his expensive, unsuccessful wars in France. He quarreled with the pope and seized church properties. The royal courts became arbitrary and capricious.

The barons became inflamed. They had had enough. They rose in overwhelming might and forced John to parley at Runnymede, on the south bank of the Thames River in southern England. They handed him their Articles of the Barons demanding the distribution of power and the legalization of political and economic liberties. They wanted him to share powers the throne had assumed over long periods of time. The astounded monarch railed, "Why don't they ask for my kingdom!" Fearing civil war, he capitulated and set his seal to the Articles. Four days of debate and compromise reduced the petition to a 63-clause document that allayed the barons' discontent: Magna Carta.

Magna Carta set out remedies for specific abuses and sought to distinguish between rule by law and rule through arbitrary power. Feudal rights were insured. The king could not encroach on baronial privileges. Royal powers relating to taxes and jurisdiction were limited in favor of the king's vassals. The freedom of the church and the customs of the towns were guaranteed. The pledged liberties ran to "all the free men of our kingdom." A year after Runnymede, John died during his renewed struggle with the barons.

Magna Carta was reconsidered clause by clause in 1217, 1225, and 1297. Confirmed and reconfirmed by generations of kings, it acquired the status of fundamental law. In the seventeenth century, the great English jurist Sir Edward Coke proclaimed, "Magna Carta is such a fellow that he will have no sovereign."

The English took Magna Carta and its principles of liberty under law with them across the Atlantic to the "new world." In the 1760s and 1770s, Americans cited Magna Carta as one of the landmarks guarding the liberties they claimed against the mother country's colonial policies.

A copy of the 1297 Magna Carta (in Latin script on parchment measuring 14½ × 17¾ inches) is on display in the rotunda of the National Archives in Washington, D.C., because the foundation for fundamental English rights includes trial by jury, equality before the law, freedom from arbitrary arrest—profoundly important individual privileges with a direct legacy in the first ten amendments to the Constitution of the United States, the Bill of Rights.

Magna Carta

John, by the grace of God, king of England, lord of Ireland, duke of Normandy and Aquitaine, and count of Anjou, to the archbishops, bishops, abbots, earls, barons, justiciars, foresters, sheriffs, stewards, servants, and to all his bailiffs and faithful subjects, greeting. Know that we, out of reverence for God and for the salvation of our soul and those of all our ancestors and heirs, for the honour of God and the exaltation of holy church, and for the reform of our realm, on the advice of our venerable fathers, Stephen, archbishop of Canterbury, primate of all England and cardinal of the holy Roman church, Henry archbishop of Dublin, William of London, Peter of Winchester, Jocelyn of Bath and Glastonbury, ... John Marshal, John fitz Hugh, and others, our faithful subjects:

[1] In the first place have granted to God, and by this our present charter confirmed for us and our heirs for ever that the English church shall be free, and shall have its rights undiminished and its liberties unimpaired; and it is our will that it be thus observed; which is evident from the fact that, before the quarrel between us and our barons began, we willingly and spontaneously granted and by our charter confirmed the freedom of elections which is reckoned most important and very essential to the English church, and obtained confirmation of it from the lord pope Innocent III; the which we will observe and we wish our heirs to observe it in good faith for ever. We have also granted to all free men of our kingdom, for ourselves and our heirs for ever, all the liberties written below, to be had and held by them and their heirs of us and our heirs.

[2] If any of our earls or barons or others holding of us in chief by knight service dies, and at his death his heir be of full age and owe relief he shall have his inheritance on payment of the old relief, namely the heir or heirs of an earl £100 for a whole earl's barony, the heir or heirs of a baron £100 for a whole barony, the heir or heirs of a knight 100s, at most, for a whole knight's fee; and he who owes less shall give less according to the ancient usage of fiefs. . . .

[7] A widow shall have her marriage portion and inheritance forthwith and without difficulty after the death of her husband; nor shall she pay anything to have her dower or her marriage portion or the inheritance which she and her husband held on the day of her husband's death; and she may remain in her husband's house for forty days after his death, within which time her dower shall be assigned to her.

[8] No widow shall be forced to marry so long as she wishes to live without a husband, provided that she gives security not to marry without our consent if she holds of us, or without the consent of her lord of whom she holds, if she holds of another.

[9] Neither we nor our bailiffs will seize for any debt any land or rent, so long as the chattels of the debtor are sufficient to repay the debt; nor will those who have gone surety for the debtor be distrained so long as

the principal debtor is himself able to pay the debt; and if the principal debtor fails to pay the debt, having nothing wherewith to pay it, then shall the sureties answer for the debt; and they shall, if they wish, have the lands and rents of the debtor until they are reimbursed for the debt which they have paid for him, unless the principal debtor can show that he has discharged his obligation in the matter to the said sureties.

[10] If anyone who has borrowed from the Jews any sum, great or small, dies before it is repaid, the debt shall not bear interest as long as the heir is under age, of whomsoever he holds; and if the debt falls into our hands, we will not take anything except the principal mentioned in the bond.

[11] And if anyone dies indebted to the Jews, his wife shall have her dower and pay nothing of that debt; and if the dead man leaves children who are under age, they shall be provided with necessaries befitting the holding of the deceased; and the debt shall be paid out of the residue, reserving, however, service due to lords of the land; debts owing to others than Jews shall be dealt with in like manner.

[12] No scutage or aid shall be imposed in our kingdom unless by common counsel of our kingdom, except for ransoming our person, for making our eldest son a knight, and for once marrying our eldest daughter, and for these only a reasonable aid shall be levied. Be it done in like manner concerning aids from the city of London.

[13] And the city of London shall have all its ancient liberties and free customs as well by land as by water. Furthermore, we will and grant that all other cities, boroughs, towns, and ports shall have all their liberties and free customs. . . .

[15] We will not in future grant any one the right to take an aid from his free men, except for ransoming his person, for making his eldest son a knight and for once marrying his eldest daughter, and for these only a reasonable aid shall be levied. . . .

[18] Recognitions of *novel disseisin,* of *mort d'ancester,* and of *darrein presentment,* shall not be held elsewhere than in the counties to which they relate, and in this manner—we, or, if we should be out of the realm, our chief justiciar, will send two justices through each county four times a year, who, with four knights of each county chosen by the county, shall hold the said assizes in the county and on the day and in the place of meeting of the county court. . . .

[20] A free man shall not be amerced for a trivial offence except in accordance with the degree of the offence, and for a grave offence he shall be amerced in accordance with its gravity, yet saving his way of living; and a merchant in the same way, saving his stock-in-trade; and a villein shall be amerced in the same way, saving his means of livelihood—if they have fallen into our mercy: and none of the aforesaid amercements shall be imposed except by the oath of good men of the neighbourhood. . . .

[23] No vill or individual shall be compelled to make bridges at river banks, except those who from of old are legally bound to do so. . . .

[27] If any free man dies without leaving a will, his chattels shall be distributed by his nearest kinsfolk and friends under the supervision of the church, saving to every one the debts which the deceased owed him.

[28] No constable or other bailiff of ours shall take anyone's corn or other chattels unless he pays on the spot in cash for them or can delay payment by arrangement with the seller.

[29] No constable shall compel any knight to give money instead of castle-guard if he is willing to do the guard himself or through another good man, if for some good reason he cannot do it himself; and if we lead or send him on military service, he shall be excused guard in proportion to the time that because of us he has been on service.

[30] No sheriff, or bailiff of ours, or anyone else shall take the horses or carts of any free man for transport work save with the agreement of that freeman.

[31] Neither we nor our bailiffs will take, for castles or other works of ours, timber which is not ours, except with the agreement of him whose timber it is. . . .

[33] Henceforth all fish-weirs shall be cleared completely from the Thames and the Medway and throughout all England, except along the sea coast. . . .

[35] Let there be one measure for wine throughout our kingdom, and one measure for ale, and one measure for corn, namely "the London quarter"; and one width for cloths whether dyed, russet or halberget, namely two ells within the selvedges. Let it be the same with weights as with measures.

[36] Nothing shall be given or taken in future for the writ of inquisition of life or limbs: instead it shall be granted free of charge and not refused. . . .

[38] No bailiff shall in future put anyone to trial upon his own bare word, without reliable witnesses produced for this purpose.

[39] No free man shall be arrested or imprisoned or disseised or outlawed or exiled or in any way victimised, neither will we attack him or send anyone to attack him, except by the lawful judgment of his peers or by the law of the land.

[40] To no one will we sell, to no one will we refuse or delay right or justice.

[41] All merchants shall be able to go out of and come into England safely and securely and stay and travel throughout England, as well by land as by water, for buying and selling by the ancient and right customs free from all evil tolls, except in time of war and if they are of the land that is at war with us. . . .

[42] It shall be lawful in future for anyone, without prejudicing the allegiance due to us, to leave our kingdom and return safely and securely by land and water, save, in the public interest, for a short period in time of war—except for those imprisoned or outlawed in accordance with the law of the kingdom and natives of a land that is at war with us and merchants (who shall be treated as aforesaid). . . .

[44] Men who live outside the forest need not henceforth come before our justices of the forest upon a general summons, unless they are impleaded or are sureties for any person or persons who are attached for forest offences. . . .

[46] All barons who have founded abbeys for which they have charters of the kings of England or ancient tenure shall have the custody of them

during vacancies, as they ought to have.

[47] All forests that have been made forest in our time shall be immediately disafforested; and so be it done with riverbanks that have been made preserves by us in our time.

[48] All evil customs connected with forests and warrens, foresters and warreners, sheriffs and their officials, riverbanks and their wardens shall immediately be inquired into in each county by twelve sworn knights of the same county who are to be chosen by good men of the same county, and within forty days of the completion of the inquiry shall be utterly abolished by them so as never to be restored, provided that we, or our justiciar if we are not in England, know of it first.

[49] We will immediately return all hostages and charters given to us by Englishmen, as security for peace or faithful service. . . .

[51] As soon as peace is restored, we will remove from the kingdom all foreign knights, cross-bowmen, serjeants, and mercenaries, who have come with horses and arms to the detriment of the kingdom.

[52] If anyone has been disseised of or kept out of his lands, castles, franchises or his right by us without the legal judgment of his peers, we will immediately restore them to him: and if a dispute arises over this, then let it be decided by the judgment of the twenty-five barons who are mentioned below in the clause for securing the peace; for all the things, however, which anyone has been disseised or kept out of without the lawful judgment of his peers by king Henry, our father, or by king Richard, our brother, which we have in our hand or are held by others, to whom we are bound to warrant them, we will have the usual period of respite of crusaders, excepting those things about which a plea was started or an inquest made by our command before we took the cross; when however we return from our pilgrimage, or if by any chance we do not go on it, we will at once do full justice therein. . . .

[54] No one shall be arrested or imprisoned upon the appeal of a woman for the death of anyone except her husband.

[55] All fines made with us unjustly and against the law of the land, and all amercements imposed unjustly and against the law of the land, shall be entirely remitted, . . .

[56] If we have disseised or kept out Welshmen from lands or liberties or other things without the legal judgment of their peers in England or in Wales, they shall be immediately restored to them; and if a dispute arises over this, then let it be decided in the March by the judgment of their peers—for holdings in England according to the law of England, for holdings in Wales according to the law of Wales, and for holdings in the March according to the law of the March. Welshmen shall do the same to us and ours. . . .

[62] And we have fully remitted and pardoned to everyone all the ill-will, indignation and rancour that have arisen between us and our men, clergy and laity, from the time of the quarrel. . . .

[63] Wherefore we wish and firmly enjoin that the English church shall be free, and that the men in our kingdom shall have and hold all the aforesaid liberties, rights and concessions well and peacefully, freely and quietly, fully and completely, for themselves and their heirs from us and our heirs, in all matters and in all places for ever, as is aforesaid. An oath, moreover, has been taken, as well on our part as on the part of the barons, that all these things aforesaid shall be observed in good faith and without evil disposition.

The Mayflower Compact

" . . . for our better ordering and preservation, . . . "

November 11, 1620

In the 1600s, Englishmen sought to make fortunes by founding colonies in North America. The principal group behind most such ventures was the Virginia Company, which issued "letters patent" authorizing the founding of colonies in the vast area of land it claimed along the eastern coast of the "new" continent. Among the colonists who received letters patent were the Separatists (whom we know as Pilgrim Fathers). These Christian dissenters from the Church of England wanted to establish their own colony, or "plantation," in America, free from the Church's religious and political authority.

Thirty-six Pilgrims who had emigrated to Leyden, Holland, welcomed sixty-six non-Pilgrims (whom they called Strangers) aboard the *Mayflower* for the voyage to America. Rough weather on the North Atlantic drove the three-masted, 90-foot-long vessel north of the territory marked out in the patent. Learning that the Pilgrims were going to make landfall along the coastline sheltered by Cape Cod in New England, the Strangers became rebellious, declaring that once ashore they "would use their owne liberties, for no one had the power to command them."

The Strangers—an "undesirable lot," the Pilgrim leader William Bradford was to write—had to be pacified. Eight days before "a good harbor and pleasant bay" (Provincetown) was sighted, the male Pilgrims and most of the male Strangers— forty-one men in all—gathered in a cabin of the whaler-slaver-wineship of 180-tons burden and struck an agreement to provide for the unity and authority of the proposed colony. The social contract, modeled on the church covenants the Pilgrims had used in England, established a "Civil Body Politic" to enact "just and equal Laws, Ordinances, Acts, Constitutions and Offices." The Mayflower Compact was dated November 11, 1620.

The document did not stand for a new philosophy of government, nor was it intended to be a constitution. Rather, it was a symbol of government by consent, foreshadowing later ideas and ideals of democratic governance. As the historian Richard Hofstadter pointed out, it exemplified "the ultimate view of the Protestant Reformation, namely, that a group of men could form their own church, a religious conviction complementing the idea that men could assemble to form their own government."

The Compact went into force six weeks after it was signed. On December 26, 1620, the *Mayflower* dropped anchor along the eastern shore of Massachusetts, and the settlers established "Plimoth Plantation" on land of the Wampanoag Indians. The colony lasted until 1686, when King James II ordered it merged into the Dominion of New England. Five years later, and after the Dominion was broken up by the Glorious Revolution, or Bloodless Revolution, which toppled the monarch, Plymouth merged with the colony of Massachusetts Bay, which had been founded in 1630 by Puritans, another group of religious dissenters.

About half of the original Plymouth settlers died from scurvy and exposure during that first winter, 1620–1621, but none of the survivors chose to return to England on the *Mayflower,* which lifted anchor on April 7, 1621. That October, Plymouth celebrated its first Thanksgiving Day. By mid-century, the colony still had fewer than 1000 inhabitants. Colonial governments in Massachusetts and offshoots in the rest of the New England woods used the Mayflower Compact as the source for their own covenants.

The original document has disappeared. The text is preserved in the classic *History of Plimouth Plantation,* written by William Bradford (1590–1657), the colony's governor for thirty one-year terms between 1622 and 1656.

The Mayflower Compact

In the name of God, Amen. We whose names are underwritten, the loyal subjects of our dread Sovereign Lord King James, by the Grace of God, of Great Britain, France, and Ireland King, Defender of the Faith, etc.

Having undertaken, for the Glory of God, and advancement of the Christian Faith, and Honour of our King and Country, a Voyage to plant the First Colony in the Northern Parts of Virginia, do by these presents solemnly and mutually in the presence of God and one of another, Covenant, and Combine ourselves together into a Civil Body Politic, for our better ordering and preservation, and furtherance of the ends aforesaid; and by virtue hereof to enact, constitute, and frame such just and equal Laws, Ordinances, Acts, Constitutions, Offices, from time to time, as shall be thought most meet and convenient for the general good of the Colony: unto which we promise all due submission and obedience. In witness whereof we have hereunder subscribed our names; Cape Cod, the 11th of November, in the year of the reign of our Sovereign Lord King James, of England, France and Ireland the eighteenth, and of Scotland the fifty-fourth. Anno Domini 1620.

The Declaration of Independence

"We hold these truths to be self-evident, . . . "

July 4, 1776

It was the first half of the year 1776. The Scottish economist Adam Smith was making *An Inquiry into the Nature and Causes of the Wealth of Nations*. The British explorer James Cook was sailing around the Pacific Ocean for the third time. Mozart was composing Serenade in D Major. The English historian Edward Gibbon was grappling with his six-volume *The History of the Decline and Fall of the Roman Empire*. Field Marshal Grigori Potemkin, a favorite of Czarina Catherine II, was organizing the Russian Black Sea fleet. The most memorable event was taking place in Great Britain's United Colonies in North America: a war to subdue the colonists' revolt against British authority was in its second year. For the colonists, it was a war of defense against British tyranny and the corruption of the British constitution with regard to colonial policies. In the small town of Philadelphia, the Second Continental Congress was turning the war into a democratic revolution. Most congressmen believed the revolution would fail unless they identified independence as its goal; it is not known how many Americans wanted to be independent.

On June 7, Richard Henry Lee of Virginia introduced three resolutions in Congress calling for independence of all thirteen colonies. Three committees were named: one to work out a plan of confederation for the colonies; one to seek alliances with foreign countries to support a war for independence; one to prepare a declaration explaining the reasons for independence.

Between June 11 and June 28, the taciturn, shy Thomas Jefferson of Virginia composed one of the two most important American state documents, the Declaration of Independence. (The Constitution of 1787 is the other.) He was selected for the task, as the forceful political theorist John Adams was to recall, because he had "a happy talent for composition and a peculiar felicity of expression." Working alone, Jefferson "turned to neither book nor paper in writing it." He later declared that his purpose had been "not to find new principles, or new arguments, never before thought of, not merely to say things which had never been said before; but to place before mankind the common sense of the subject, in terms so plain and firm as to command their assent, and to justify ourselves in the independent stand we are compelled to take . . . and to give that expression the proper tone and spirit called for by the occasion . . . The Declaration was intended to be an expression of the American mind."

On July 2, Congress declared "that these United Colonies are, and of right ought to be, free and independent States, that they are absolved from all allegiance to the British Crown, . . . " Writing the next day to his wife, Abigail, Adams rejoiced: "The Second Day of July, 1776, will be the most memorable Epocha in

the History of America . . . It ought to be commemorated . . . It ought to be solemnized with Pomp and Parade, with Shews, Games, Sports, Guns, Bells, Bonfires, and Illuminations from one end of this Continent to the other from this Time forward forever more." He was right about everything except the date. There was some editing to be done. Congress adopted the Declaration of Independence on July 4.

Enumerating grievances against the Crown and asserting American ideals, the document became the great American symbol of independence, revolution, and liberty. It was the capstone of the war of words that the colonists had waged with Great Britain for more than a decade. Because Congress had given up on trying to persuade Parliament, the target of its earliest addresses and declarations, the Declaration makes only one indirect reference to Parliament. Its preamble stated the basic principles on which the Americans grounded their revolution and their new forms of government. Its body presented a long, eloquent indictment of George III for breaching his responsibilities under the English constitution to his subjects in his former colonies.

Despite the painting and engravings by John Trumbull, only the president of Congress, John Hancock of Massachusetts, signed the Declaration on July 4; most of the other fifty-five signers added their names on August 2, toasting the event with Madeira, the colonists' favorite wine, and hailing the "self-evident truth" that "whenever any Form of Government becomes destructive of [unalienable rights, which include life, liberty, and the pursuit of happiness], it is the Right of the People to alter or to abolish it, and to institute new Government, laying its foundation on such principles and organizing its powers in such form, as to them shall seem most likely to effect their Safety and Happiness." A few delegates signed as late as mid-1777.

The original parchment, damaged by the making of a facsimile in 1819 and by years of display in direct sunlight in the Library of Congress, rests today in a protective steel-and-bulletproof glass case, filled with inert gases, in the National Archives, in Washington, D.C.

The Revolutionary War lasted until Britain formally acknowledged the independence of the United States in the Treaty of Paris, 1783.

The Declaration of Independence

IN CONGRESS, JULY 4, 1776

THE UNANIMOUS DECLARATION OF THE THIRTEEN UNITED STATES OF AMERICA,

When in the Course of human events, it becomes necessary for one people to dissolve the political bands which have connected them with another, and to assume among the Powers of the earth, the separate and equal station to which the Laws of Nature and of Nature's God entitle them, a decent respect to the opinions of mankind requires that they should declare the causes which impel them to the separation.

We hold these truths to be self-evident, that all men are created equal, that they are endowed by their Creator with certain unalienable Rights, that among these are Life, Liberty and the pursuit of Happiness. That to secure these rights, Governments are instituted among Men, deriving their just powers from the consent of the governed. That whenever any Form of Government becomes destructive of these ends, it is the Right of the People to alter or to abolish it, and to institute new Government, laying its foundation on such principles and organizing its powers in such form, as to them shall seem most likely to effect their Safety and Happiness. Prudence, indeed, will dictate that Governments long established should not be changed for light and transient causes; and accordingly all experience hath shown, that mankind are more disposed to suffer, while evils are sufferable, than to right themselves by abolishing the forms to which they are accustomed. But when a long train of abuses and usurpations, pursuing invariably the same Object evinces a design to reduce them under absolute Despotism, it is their right, it is their duty, to throw off such Government, and to provide new Guards for their future security.—Such has been the patient sufferance of these Colonies; and such is now the necessity which constrains them to alter their former Systems of Government. The history of the present King of Great Britain is a history of repeated injuries and usurpations, all having in direct object the establishment of an absolute Tyranny over these States. To prove this, let Facts be submitted to a candid world.

He has refused his Assent to Laws, the most wholesome and necessary for the public good.

He has forbidden his Governors to pass Laws of immediate and pressing importance, unless suspended in their operation till his Assent should be obtained; and when so suspended, he has utterly neglected to attend to them.

He has refused to pass other Laws for the accommodation of large

districts of people, unless those people would relinquish the right of Representation in the Legislature, a right inestimable to them and formidable to tyrants only.

He has called together legislative bodies at places unusual, uncomfortable, and distant from the depository of their Public Records, for the sole purpose of fatiguing them into compliance with his measures.

He has dissolved Representative Houses repeatedly, for opposing with manly firmness his invasions on the rights of the people.

He has refused for a long time, after such dissolutions, to cause others to be elected; whereby the Legislative Powers, incapable of Annihilation, have returned to the People at large for their exercise; the State remaining in the mean time exposed to all the dangers of invasion from without, and convulsions within.

He has endeavoured to prevent the population of these States; for that purpose obstructing the Laws of Naturalization of Foreigners; refusing to pass others to encourage their migration hither, and raising the conditions of new Appropriations of Lands.

He has obstructed the Administration of Justice, by refusing his Assent to Laws for establishing Judiciary Powers.

He has made Judges dependent on his Will alone, for the tenure of their offices, and the amount and payment of their salaries.

He has erected a multitude of New Offices, and sent hither swarms of Officers to harass our People, and eat out their substance.

He has kept among us, in times of peace, Standing Armies without the Consent of our legislature.

He has affected to render the Military independent of and superior to the Civil Power.

He has combined with others to subject us to a jurisdiction foreign to our constitution, and unacknowledged by our laws; giving his Assent to their acts of pretended legislation:

For quartering large bodies of armed troops among us:

For protecting them, by a mock Trial, from Punishment for any Murders which they should commit on the Inhabitants of these States:

For cutting off our Trade with all parts of the world:

For imposing taxes on us without our Consent:

For depriving us in many cases, of the benefits of Trial by Jury:

For transporting us beyond Seas to be tried for pretended offences:

For abolishing the free System of English Laws in a neighbouring Province, establishing therein an Arbitrary government, and enlarging its Boundaries so as to render it at once an example and fit instrument for introducing the same absolute rule into these Colonies:

For taking away our Charters, abolishing our most valuable Laws, and altering fundamentally the Forms of our Governments:

For suspending our own Legislature, and declaring themselves invested with Power to legislate for us in all cases whatsoever.

He has abdicated Government here, by declaring us out of his Protection and waging War against us.

He has plundered our seas, ravaged our Coasts, burnt our towns, and destroyed the lives of our people.

He is at this time transporting large armies of foreign mercenaries to compleat the works of death, desolation and tyranny, already begun with circumstances of Cruelty & perfidy scarcely paralleled in the most barbarous ages, and totally unworthy the Head of a civilized nation.

He has constrained our fellow Citizens taken Captive on the high Seas to bear Arms against their Country, to become the executioners of their friends and Brethren, or to fall themselves by their Hands.

He has excited domestic insurrections amongst us, and has endeavoured to bring on the inhabitants of our frontiers, the merciless Indian Savages, whose known rule of warfare, is an undistinguished destruction of all ages, sexes and conditions.

In every stage of these Oppressions We have Petitioned for Redress in the most humble terms: Our repeated Petitions have been answered only by repeated injury. A Prince, whose character is thus marked by every act which may define a Tyrant, is unfit to be the ruler of a free People.

Nor have We been wanting in attention to our British brethren. We have warned them from time to time of attempts by their legislature to extend an unwarrantable jurisdiction over us. We have reminded them of the circumstances of our emigration and settlement here. We have appealed to their native justice and magnanimity, and we have conjured them by the ties of our common kindred to disavow these usurpations, which, would inevitably interrupt our connections and correspondence. They too have been deaf to the voice of justice and of consanguinity. We must, therefore, acquiesce in the necessity, which denounces our Separation, and hold them, as we hold the rest of mankind, Enemies in War, in Peace Friends.

We, therefore, the Representatives of the united States of America, in General Congress, Assembled, appealing to the Supreme Judge of the world for the rectitude of our intentions, do, in the Name, and by Authority of the good People of these Colonies, solemnly publish and declare, That these United Colonies are, and of Right ought to be Free and Independent States; that they are Absolved from all Allegiance to the British Crown, and that all political connection between them and the State of Great Britain, is and ought to be totally dissolved; and that as Free and Independent States, they have full Power to levy War, conclude Peace, contract Alliances, establish Commerce, and to do all other Acts and Things which Independent States may of right do. And for the support of this Declaration, with a firm reliance on the Protection of Divine Providence, we mutually pledge to each other our Lives, our Fortunes and our sacred Honor.

JOHN HANCOCK

New Hampshire
JOSIAH BARTLETT,
WM. WHIPPLE,
MATTHEW THORNTON.

Massachusetts-Bay
SAML. ADAMS,
JOHN ADAMS,
ROBT. TREAT PAINE,
ELBRIDGE GERRY.

Rhode Island
STEP. HOPKINS,
WILLIAM ELLERY.

Connecticut
ROGER SHERMAN,
SAM'EL HUNTINGTON,
WM. WILLIAMS,
OLIVER WOLCOTT.

New York
WM. FLOYD,
PHIL. LIVINGSTON,
FRANS. LEWIS,
LEWIS MORRIS.

Pennsylvania
ROBT. MORRIS,
BENJAMIN RUSH,
BENJA. FRANKLIN,
JOHN MORTON,
GEO. CLYMER,
JAS. SMITH,
GEO. TAYLOR,
JAMES WILSON,
GEO. ROSS.

Delaware
CAESAR RODNEY,
GEO. READ,
THO. M'KEAN.

North Carolina
Wm. Hooper,
Joseph Hewes,
John Penn.

South Carolina
Edward Rutledge,
Thos. Heyward, Junr.,
Thomas Lynch, Junr.,
Arthur Middleton.

New Jersey
Richd. Stockton,
Jno. Witherspoon,
Fras. Hopkinson,
John Hart,
Abra. Clark.

Georgia
Button Gwinnett,
Lyman Hall,
Geo. Walton.

Maryland
Samuel Chase,
Wm. Paca,
Thos. Stone,
Charles Carroll of Carrollton.

Virginia
George Wythe,
Richard Henry Lee,
Th. Jefferson,
Benja. Harrison,
Ths. Nelson, Jr.,
Francis Lightfoot Lee,
Carter Braxton.

The U.S. Bill of Rights

" . . . no law . . . abridging the freedom of speech, or of the press; . . . "

December 15, 1791

The U.S. Bill of Rights was an afterthought. It was only in the last week of the four-month Federal Convention in Philadelphia in 1787 that a provision protecting the rights of the individual against the powers of the proposed national government was even introduced for inclusion in the constitution being composed. Most of the delegates argued that the government would have no power to harm individual rights—state constitutions already protected those rights. Also, the attempt to write a federal declaration would be more trouble than it was worth—delegates were exhausted and wanted to go home. But three advocates of a bill of rights refused to sign the Constitution before it was dispatched with thirty-nine signatures to the nascent, fragile, debt-ridden country's Confederation Congress in New York. Eight days later, the Congress reluctantly sent copies of the four pages of prescient parchment to ratifying conventions called by the legislatures of twelve of the thirteen states.

Opponents of the Constitution, who were known as Grumbletonians, argued that the strong federal government designed by the Constitution would become a tyranny without a bill of rights. Supporters of the Constitution, Federalists such as James Madison, realized that ratification of the charter might fail without a strategic compromise: conceding that "the supreme law of the land" might indeed need some adjustment, they promised to work for a bill of rights in the First Congress, and urged the ratifying conventions to recommend versions of such amendments to Congress. The proposal gave "great quiet to the people." Still, North Carolina announced it would not ratify the Constitution until Congress had actually presented a bill of rights; Virginia and New York ratified the Constitution with the stipulation that the First Congress must add a bill of rights; Rhode Island, which had not sent even a single delegate to the Federal Convention, didn't bother to call a convention to adopt the charter.

On June 8, 1789, Representative Madison of Virginia challenged Congress to redeem the Federalists' pledge to the people. He offered a set of amendments that he had drawn from the 210 proposals submitted by the ratifying conventions. After nearly four months of debate, Congress sent a dozen to the states. By December 15, 1791, eleven of the fourteen states had ratified ten—the Bill of Rights— amending the Constitution for the first time. (Two technical amendments, having to do with the size of the House of Representatives and the salary of Congress, were not adopted; only sixteen more amendments have been adopted in the last two centuries.)

The "majestic generalities" of the Bill of Rights reserve to the people or to the states power not delegated to the federal government. Their roots were in English history, the political traditions of the colonies, state constitutions of the 1770s and 1780s, and the idealistic political theory of the Enlightenment. The First Amendment protects the free exercise of religious belief and forbids official endorsement of religion; it also guards freedom of speech, press, assembly, and petition. The controversial Second Amendment protects either an individual's right to keep and bear arms or state governments' authority to raise and support "a well-regulated Militia" independent of federal control except in times of special danger. The Third Amendment, which bars the quartering of soldiers in citizens' homes, responded to British abuses in the years before independence. The Fourth, Fifth, Sixth, and Eighth Amendments protect individual rights in the process by which government investigates, prosecutes, and punishes violations of law. The Seventh Amendment protects the right to trial by jury in non-criminal lawsuits in federal courts. The Ninth Amendment protects rights that are not specified in the other amendments, though the courts disagree on how to make use of it. The Tenth Amendment stands for the ideas of limited government and federalism.

For most of its history, the Bill of Rights was held to limit only the federal government. In 1925, the Supreme Court began a process known as "incorporation"; the justices held that the due process clause of the Fourteenth Amendment (adopted in 1868) applies some clauses of the federal Bill of Rights to limit the powers of state and local government. "The safeguards of liberty," Supreme Court Justice Felix Frankfurter observed, "have frequently been forged in controversies involving not very nice people."

Fourteen engrossed parchment originals of the Bill of Rights were prepared in 1789; eleven survive today, one on permanent display in the National Archives, in Washington, D.C.

The Bill of Rights

AMENDMENTS TO THE CONSTITUTION
OF THE UNITED STATES OF AMERICA

(The first ten amendments—the Bill of Rights—were ratified in 1791, 1 year, 2½ months after being sent to the states for ratification.)

Amendment 1
FREEDOM OF RELIGION, SPEECH, AND THE PRESS; RIGHT OF ASSEMBLY
Congress shall make no law respecting an establishment of religion, or prohibiting the free exercise thereof; or abridging the freedom of speech, or of the press; or the right of the people peaceably to assemble, and to petition the government for a redress of grievances.

Amendment 2
RIGHT TO KEEP AND BEAR ARMS
A well-regulated militia, being necessary to the security of a free State, the right of the people to keep and bear arms, shall not be infringed.

Amendment 3
QUARTERING OF TROOPS
No soldier shall, in time of peace be quartered in any house, without the consent of the owner, nor in time of war, but in a manner to be prescribed by law.

Amendment 4
LIMITING THE RIGHT OF SEARCH
The right of the people to be secure in their persons, houses, papers, and effects, against unreasonable searches and seizures, shall not be violated, and no warrants shall issue but upon probable cause, supported

by oath or affirmation, and particularly describing the place to be searched, and the persons or things to be seized.

Amendment 5
GUARANTY OF TRIAL BY JURY; PRIVATE PROPERTY TO BE RESPECTED
No person shall be held to answer for a capital, or otherwise infamous crime, unless on a presentment or indictment of a grand jury, except in cases arising in the land or naval forces, or in the militia, when in actual service in time of war or public danger; nor shall any person be subject for the same offense to be twice put in jeopardy of life or limb; nor shall be compelled in any criminal case to be a witness against himself, nor be deprived of life, liberty, or property, without due process of law; nor shall private property be taken for public use, without just compensation.

Amendment 6
RIGHTS OF ACCUSED PERSONS
In all criminal prosecutions, the accused shall enjoy the right to a speedy and public trial, by an impartial jury of the State and district wherein the crime shall have been committed, which districts shall have been previously ascertained by law, and to be informed of the nature and cause of the accusation; to be confronted with the witnesses against him; to have compulsory process for obtaining witnesses in his favor, and to have the assistance of counsel for his defense.

Amendment 7
RULES OF THE COMMON LAW
In suits at common law, where the value in controversy shall exceed twenty dollars, the right of trial by jury shall be preserved, and no fact tried by a jury, shall be otherwise re-examined in any court of the United States than according to the rules of common law.

Amendment 8
EXCESSIVE BAIL, FINES, AND PUNISHMENT PROHIBITED
Excessive bail shall not be required, nor excessive fines imposed, nor cruel and unusual punishments inflicted.

Amendment 9
RIGHTS RETAINED BY THE PEOPLE
The enumeration in the Constitution of certain rights shall not be construed to deny or disparage others retained by the people.

Amendment 10
POWERS RESERVED TO STATES AND PEOPLE
The powers not delegated to the United States by the Constitution, nor prohibited by it to the States, are reserved to the States respectively, or to the people.

Washington's Farewell Address

"Cultivate peace and harmony . . ."

September 19, 1796

The September 19, 1796, issue of the noted Philadelphia printer David Claypoole's *American Daily Advertiser* dropped a political bombshell on the American people. Under a small headline on the second and third pages of the four-page newspaper, President George Washington announced that he would not seek or accept a third four-year term. The message was much more than a notice of his retirement (and the beginning of a political tradition—no third term—that would last nearly a century and a half). He intended the Farewell Address to be his valedictory—explaining and justifying his policies and his conduct in office, marking out the virtuous path he urged his countrymen to follow, leading the rest of the globe to liberty.

Washington never wanted to be chief executive. After the eight-year Revolutionary War, he had retired to his Virginia plantation overlooking the Potomac River, determined to live out his days as the Squire of Mount Vernon. But he saw the "perpetual Union" of the thirteen former colonies "always moving upon crutches and tottering at every step," a crippled ship of state. In 1787, he deemed it to be his duty to attend the Federal Convention in Philadelphia, where the Articles of Confederation might be revised. "To see this country happy," he said, "is so much the wish of my soul." The four-month convention and the framing of an entirely new charter—Washington was the presiding officer—would have been doomed without his participation. Less than two years later, he again heard the venerating voice of his countrymen and the entreaties of his friends and political allies, this time beseeching him to accept the electors' unanimous decision to make him the first president of the United States under the new Constitution.

Toward the end of his first term, Washington was made sick at heart by the partisan bickering that threatened to rip his administration asunder, and he decided to retire. He asked his longtime adviser, Representative James Madison of Virginia, to draft a farewell message. Only the pleas of Secretary of State Thomas Jefferson and Secretary of the Treasury Alexander Hamilton—who could agree on nothing else—persuaded Washington to accept a second term.

But four years later, Washington was fed up. Party strife between Federalists and Republicans, between backers of revolutionary France and advocates of Great Britain, between friends of a commercial economy and supporters of a farming economy, exhausted and embittered him. He took much of the "phrenzy of party" personally; he could not distinguish criticism of his policies from attacks on him.

Washington retrieved the draft prepared by Madison in 1792 and sent it to Hamilton in New York with a letter outlining his thoughts on what his last message to the country should say. Hamilton and Washington passed drafts of the evolving message back and forth. Recasting Hamilton's polished version in his own words, Washington wrote out a clean copy and gave it to the printer Claypoole, asking him to publish it in his newspaper. When the address appeared three days later—which was less than two months before the election and a half year before his second term was to end—Washington was in his carriage heading for Mount Vernon and a congenial retirement. (He returned only briefly to Philadelphia, where the capital would remain until the District of Columbia was ready for occupancy at the end of the decade.)

The Farewell Address was a product of its time. Washington had been determined to vindicate his administration and he was bitter at his critics. He warned Americans against "permanent alliances" with foreign powers, a large public debt, a large military establishment, and devices of a "small, artful, enterprising minority" to control or change government. With the passage of time, the Farewell Address became a talisman by which later generations measured American politics and foreign policy.

Washington's Farewell Address

Friends and Fellow-Citizens:

The period for a new election of a citizen to administer the Executive Government of the United States being not far distant, and the time actually arrived when your thoughts must be employed in designating the person who is to be clothed with that important trust, it appears to me proper, especially as it may conduce to a more distinct expression of the public voice, that I should now apprise you of the resolution I have formed to decline being considered among the number of those out of whom a choice is to be made. . . .

The impressions with which I first undertook the arduous trust were explained on the proper occasion. In the discharge of this trust I will only say that I have, with good intentions, contributed toward the organization and administration of the Government the best exertions of which a very fallible judgment was capable. Not unconscious in the outset of the inferiority of my qualifications, experience in my own eyes, perhaps still more in the eyes of others, has strengthened the motives to diffidence of myself; and every day the increasing weight of years admonishes me more and more that the shade of retirement is as necessary to me as it will be welcome. Satisfied that if any circumstances have given peculiar value to my services they were temporary, I have the consolation to believe that, while choice and prudence invite me to quit the political scene, patriotism does not forbid it. . . .

Here, perhaps, I ought to stop. But a solicitude for your welfare which can not end with my life, and the apprehension of danger natural to that solicitude, urge me on an occasion like the present to offer to your solemn contemplation and to recommend to your frequent review some sentiments which are the result of much reflection, of no inconsiderable observation, and which appear to me all important to the permanency of your felicity as a people. . . .

The unity of government which constitutes you one people is also now dear to you. It is justly so, for it is a main pillar in the edifice of your real independence, the support of your tranquillity at home, your peace abroad, of your safety, of your prosperity, of that very liberty which you so highly prize. But as it is easy to foresee that from different causes and from different quarters much pains will be taken, many artifices employed, to weaken in your minds the conviction of this truth, as this is the point in your political fortress against which the batteries of internal and external enemies will be most constantly and actively (though often covertly and insidiously) directed, it is of infinite moment that you should properly estimate the immense value of your national union to your collective and individual happiness; that you should cherish a cordial, habitual, and immovable attachment to it; accustoming yourselves to think and speak of it as of the palladium of your political safety and prosperity; watching for its preservation with jealous anxiety; discountenancing whatever may suggest even a suspicion that it can in any event be abandoned, and indignantly frowning upon the first dawning of every attempt to alienate any portion of our country from the rest or to enfeeble the sacred ties which now link together the various parts.

. . . The name of American, which belongs to you in your national capacity, must always exalt the just pride of patriotism more than any appellation derived from local discriminations. With slight shades of difference, you have the same religion, manners, habits, and political principles. You have in a common cause fought and triumphed together. The independence and liberty you possess are the work of joint councils and joint efforts, of common dangers, sufferings, and successes.

But these considerations, however powerfully they address themselves to your sensibility, are greatly outweighed by those which apply more immediately to your interest. Here every portion of our country finds the most commanding motives for carefully guarding and preserving the union of the whole.

The *North,* in an unrestrained intercourse with the *South,* protected by the equal laws of a common government, finds in the productions of the latter great additional resources of maritime and commercial enterprise and precious materials of manufacturing industry. The *South,* in the same intercourse, benefiting by the same agency of the *North,* sees its agriculture grow and its commerce expand. Turning partly into its own channels the seamen of the *North,* it finds its particular navigation invigorated; and while it contributes in different ways to nourish and increase the general mass of the national navigation, it looks forward to the protection of a maritime strength to which itself is unequally adapted. The *East,* in a like intercourse with the *West,* already finds, and in the progressive improvement of interior communications by land and water will more and more find, a valuable vent for the commodities which it brings from abroad or manufactures at home. The *West* derives from the *East* supplies requisite to its growth and comfort, and what is perhaps of still greater consequence, it must of necessity owe the *secure* enjoyment of indispensable *outlets* for its own productions to the weight, influence, and the future maritime strength of the Atlantic side of the Union, directed by an indissoluble community of interest as one *nation.* Any other tenure by which the *West* can hold this essential advantage, whether derived from its own separate strength or from an apostate and unnatural connection with any foreign power, must be intrinsically precarious. . . .

Is there a doubt whether a common government can embrace so large a sphere? Let experience solve it. To listen to mere speculation in such a case were criminal. It is well worth a fair and full experiment. With such powerful and obvious motives to union affecting all parts of our country, while experience shall not have demonstrated its impracticability, there will always be reason to distrust the patriotism of those who in any quarter may endeavor to weaken its bands. . . .

To the efficacy and permanency of your union a government for the whole is indispensable. No alliances, however strict, between the parts can be an adequate substitute. They must inevitably experience the infractions and interruptions which all alliances in all times have experienced. Sensible of this momentous truth, you have improved upon your first essay by the adoption of a Constitution of Government better calculated than your former for an intimate union and for the efficacious management of your common concerns. This Government, the offspring of our own choice, uninfluenced and unawed, adopted upon full investigation and mature deliberation, completely free in its principles, in the distribution of its powers, uniting security with energy, and containing within itself a provision for its own amendment, has a just claim to your confidence and your support. Respect for its authority, compliance with its laws, acquiescence in its measures, are duties enjoined by the fundamental maxims of true liberty. The basis of our political systems is the right of the people to make and to alter their constitutions of government. But the constitution which at any time exists till changed by an explicit and authentic act of the whole people is sacredly obligatory upon all. The very idea of the power and the right of the people to establish government presupposes the duty of every individual to obey the established government. . . .

Toward the preservation of your Government and the permanency of your present happy state, it is requisite not only that you steadily discountenance irregular oppositions to its acknowledged authority, but also that you resist with care the spirit of innovation upon its principles, however specious the pretexts. One method of assault may be to effect in the forms of the Constitution alterations which will impair the energy of the system, and thus to undermine what can not be directly overthrown. In all the changes to which you may be invited remember that time and habit are at least as necessary to fix the true character of governments as of other human institutions; that experience is the surest standard by which to test the real tendency of the existing constitution of a country; that facility in changes upon the credit of mere hypothesis and opinion exposes to perpetual change, from the endless variety of hypothesis and opinion; and remember especially that for the efficient management of your common interests in a country so extensive as ours a government of as much vigor as is consistent with the perfect security of liberty is indispensable. Liberty itself will find in such a government, with powers properly distributed and adjusted, its surest guardian. It is, indeed, little else than a name where the government is too feeble to withstand the enterprises of faction, to confine each member of the society within the limits prescribed by the laws, and to maintain all in the secure and tranquil enjoyment of the rights of person and property.

I have already intimated to you the danger of parties in the State, with particular reference to the founding of them on geographical discriminations. Let me now take a more comprehensive view, and warn you in the most solemn manner against the baneful effects of the spirit of party generally.

This spirit, unfortunately, is inseparable from our nature, having its root in the strongest passions of the human mind. It exists under different shapes in all governments, more or less stifled, controlled, or repressed; but in those of the popular form it is seen in its greatest rankness and is truly their worst enemy. . . .

It serves always to distract the public councils and enfeeble the public administration. It agitates the community with ill-founded jealousies and false alarms; kindles the animosity of one part against another: foments occasionally riot and insurrection. It opens the door to foreign influence and corruption, which find a facilitated access to the government itself through the channels of party passion. Thus the policy and the will of one country are subjected to the policy and will of another. . . .

It is important, likewise, that the habits of thinking in a free country should inspire caution in those intrusted with its administration to confine themselves within their respective constitutional spheres, avoiding in the exercise of the powers of one department to encroach upon another. The spirit of encroachment tends to consolidate the powers of all the departments in one, and thus to create, whatever the form of government, a real despotism. . . . If in the opinion of the people the distribution or modification of the constitutional powers be in any particular wrong, let it be corrected by an amendment in the way which the Constitution designates. But let there be no change by usurpation; for though this in one instance may be the instrument of good, it is the customary weapon by which free governments are destroyed. The precedent must always greatly overbalance in permanent evil any partial or transient benefit which the use can at any time yield.

Of all the dispositions and habits which lead to political prosperity, religion and morality are indispensable supports. In vain would that man claim the tribute of patriotism who should labor to subvert these great pillars of human happiness—these firmest props of the duties of men and citizens. The mere politician, equally with the pious man, ought to respect and to cherish them. A volume could not trace all their connections with private and public felicity. Let it simply be asked, Where is the security for property, for reputation, for life, if the sense of religious obligation *desert* the oaths which are the instruments of investigation in courts of justice? And let us with caution indulge the supposition that morality can be maintained without religion. Whatever may be conceded to the influence of refined education on minds of peculiar structure, reason and experience both forbid us to expect that national morality can prevail in exclusion of religious principle.

It is substantially true that virtue or morality is a necessary spring of popular government. The rule indeed extends with more or less force to every species of free government. Who that is a sincere friend to it can look with indifference upon attempts to shake the foundation of the fabric? Promote, then, as an object of primary importance, institutions for the general diffusion of knowledge. In proportion as the structure of a government gives force to public opinion, it is essential that public opinion should be enlightened.

As a very important source of strength and security, cherish public credit. One method of preserving it is to use it as sparingly as possible, avoiding occasions of expense by cultivating peace, but remembering also that timely disbursements to prepare for danger frequently prevent much greater disbursements to repel it; avoiding likewise the accumula-

tion of debt, not only by shunning occasions of expense, but by vigorous exertions in time of peace to discharge the debts which unavoidable wars have occasioned, not ungenerously throwing upon posterity the burthen which we ourselves ought to bear. . . .

Observe good faith and justice toward all nations. Cultivate peace and harmony with all. Religion and morality enjoin this conduct. And can it be that good policy does not equally enjoin it? It will be worthy of a free, enlightened, and at no distant period a great nation to give to mankind the magnanimous and too novel example of a people always guided by an exalted justice and benevolence. Who can doubt that in the course of time and things the fruits of such a plan would richly repay any temporary advantages which might be lost by a steady adherence to it? Can it be that Providence has not connected the permanent felicity of a nation with its virtue? The experiment, at least, is recommended by every sentiment which ennobles human nature. Alas! is it rendered impossible by its vices? . . .

Against the insidious wiles of foreign influence (I conjure you to believe me, fellow-citizens) the jealousy of a free people ought to be *constantly* awake, since history and experience prove that foreign influence is one of the most baneful foes of republican government. But that jealousy, to be useful, must be impartial, else it becomes the instrument of the very influence to be avoided, instead of a defense against it. Excessive partiality for one foreign nation and excessive dislike of another cause those whom they actuate to see danger only on one side, and serve to veil and even second the arts of influence on the other. Real patriots who may resist the intrigues of the favorite are liable to become suspected and odious, while its tools and dupes usurp the applause and confidence of the people to surrender their interests. . . .

It is our true policy to steer clear of permanent alliances with any portion of the foreign world, so far, I mean, as we are now at liberty to do it; for let me not be understood as capable of patronizing infidelity to existing engagements. I hold the maxim no less applicable to public than to private affairs that honesty is always the best policy. I repeat, therefore, let those engagements be observed in their genuine sense. But in my opinion it is unnecessary and would be unwise to extend them.

Taking care always to keep ourselves by suitable establishments on a respectable defensive posture, we may safely trust to temporary alliances for extraordinary emergencies.

Harmony, liberal intercourse with all nations are recommended by policy, humanity, and interest. But even our commercial policy should hold an equal and impartial hand neither seeking nor granting exclusive favors or preferences; consulting the natural course of things; diffusing and diversifying by gentle means the streams of commerce, but forcing nothing; establishing with powers so disposed, in order to give trade a stable course to define the rights of our merchants, and to enable the Government to support them, conventional rules of intercourse, the best that present circumstances and mutual opinion will permit, but temporary and liable to be from time to time abandoned or varied as experience and circumstances shall dictate; constantly keeping in view that it is folly in one nation to look for disinterested favors from another; that it must pay with a portion of its independence for whatever it may accept under that character; that by such acceptance it may place itself in the condition of having given equivalents for nominal favors, and yet of being reproached with ingratitude for not giving more. There can be no greater error than to expect or calculate upon real favors from nation to nation. It is an illusion which experience must cure, which a just pride ought to discard. . . .

Relying on its kindness in this as in other things, and actuated by that fervent love toward it which is so natural to a man who views in it the native soil of himself and his progenitors for several generations, I anticipate with pleasing expectation that retreat in which I promise myself to realize without alloy the sweet enjoyment of partaking in the midst of my fellow-citizens the benign influence of good laws under a free government—the ever-favorite object of my heart, and the happy reward, as I trust, of our mutual cares, labors, and dangers.

G^{o.} WASHINGTON.

The Emancipation Proclamation

" . . . sincerely believed to be an act of justice . . . "

January 1, 1863

Throughout his career, Abraham Lincoln wrestled with the contradiction posed by a republic devoted to liberty that permitted one human being to own another. Slavery had bedeviled the making of the Constitution three score and fifteen years earlier and the westward expansion, the "manifest destiny," of the new country. As the nineteenth century progressed, the controversy deepened and worsened. With Lincoln's election as the first Republican president, Southern politicians became convinced that slavery would probably be destroyed. They determined to pull their states out of the Union rather than permit the ruination of the "peculiar institution."

Lincoln despised slavery, but his goal was to halt its enlargement. When angry Southerners in eleven states indeed voted to secede from the Union, the president stood firm to preserve the Union. War erupted in April 1861.

In the summer of 1862, news from the battlefields had gone, in Lincoln's words, "from bad to worse." The North "must change our tactics," the president told his cabinet, "or lose the game." In July, he drafted a proclamation freeing the slaves in the Confederate states, but was persuaded by his enthusiastic cabinet to wait for an appropriate time—a military success!—to issue the document, otherwise "it could be viewed as the last measure of an exhausted government, a cry for help."

On August 22, Lincoln publicly served notice that he was considering emancipation as a war measure. In a letter to Horace Greeley of the New York *Tribune,* he declared: "My paramount object in this struggle is to save the Union, and is not either to save or to destroy slavery. If I could save the Union without freeing *any* slave, I would do it, and if I could save it by freeing *all* the slaves I would do it; and if I could save it by freeing some and leaving others alone I would also do that. What I do about slavery, and the colored race, I do because I believe it helps to save the Union; and what I forbear, I forbear because I do *not* believe it would help to save the Union."

The decisive victory that the cabinet had wanted came on September 17, the seventy-fifth anniversary of the signing of the Constitution. The Battle of Antietam, which drove the rebels out of Maryland and back into the territory of the Confederacy, gave Lincoln the opportunity to issue the proclamation. Five days later, Lincoln announced to his cabinet his preliminary Emancipation Proclamation, under which, as of January 1, 1863, all slaves in any territory in rebellion against the United States "shall be then, thenceforward, and forever free." (There were well over 3 million slaves in the Confederacy.) Excluded from emancipation were the 450,000 slaves in Delaware, Kentucky, Maryland, and Missouri, border states that had remained within the Union; the 275,000 slaves in Union-occupied Tennessee; and myriad more in portions of Virginia and Louisiana under the control of federal armies. Slavery would not survive a final Union victory.

Morale in the North was boosted tremendously, despite widespread criticism from Southern sympathizers—Copperheads—who were opposed to a war fought for the purpose of freeing the slaves: They claimed the *abolitionists* were the reason for the bloodiest war in the history of the Western hemisphere. The Northern army was now an army of liberation, and blacks of "suitable condition" were enlisted. Throughout the South, which feared servile insurrections, disaffection bred and spread. Britain and France decided not to intervene on behalf of the Southern states, with which they had been in affinity, thus easing foreign pressure on the Lincoln Administration. The brief document gave the Union military the semblance of a moral crusade.

Lincoln signed the Emancipation Proclamation as promised, on January 1, 1863, after spending most of the day welcoming guests to the traditional New Year's reception in the White House.

Lincoln had believed that black and white Americans could not live peacefully in the same country, and had made halting suggestions that freed slaves be resettled in Africa or Central America and that slaveowners receive compensation from the federal government for their lost property. But by the time he signed the Proclamation, he had changed his mind about his earlier ideas, and pressure in Congress was mounting for a constitutional amendment to root out slavery once and for all. The Thirteenth Amendment, proposed by Congress on February 1, 1865, two months before the end of the war, was ratified at year's end, eight months after Appomattox and Lincoln's murder. Eight former slave states ratified the amendment as the price for being restored to full status within the Union.

The Emancipation Proclamation

BY THE PRESIDENT OF THE UNITED STATES OF AMERICA:

A Proclamation.

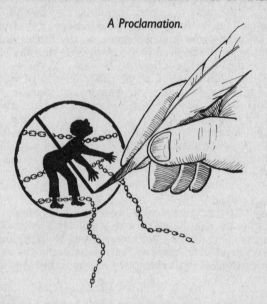

Whereas on the 22d day of September, A.D. 1862, a proclamation was issued by the President of the United States, containing, among other things, the following, to wit:

"That on the 1st day of January, A.D. 1863, all persons held as slaves within any State or designated part of a State the people whereof shall then be in rebellion against the United States shall be then, thenceforward, and forever free; and the executive government of the United States, including the military and naval authority thereof, will recognize and maintain the freedom of such persons and will do no act or acts to repress such persons, or any of them, in any efforts they may make for their actual freedom.

"That the executive will on the 1st day of January aforesaid, by proclamation, designate the States and parts of States, if any, in which the people thereof, respectively, shall then be in rebellion against the United States; and the fact that any State or the people thereof shall on that day be in good faith represented in the Congress of the United States by members chosen thereto at elections wherein a majority of the qualified voters of such States shall have participated shall, in the absence of strong countervailing testimony, be deemed conclusive evidence that such State and the people thereof are not then in rebellion against the United States."

Now, therefore, I, Abraham Lincoln, President of the United States, by virtue of the power in me vested as Commander-in-Chief of the Army and Navy of the United States in time of actual armed rebellion against the authority and government of the United States, and as a fit and necessary war measure for suppressing said rebellion, do, on this 1st day of January, A.D. 1863, and in accordance with my purpose so to do, publicly proclaimed for the full period of one hundred days from the first day above mentioned, order and designate as the States and parts of States wherein the people thereof, respectively, are this day in rebellion against the United States the following, to wit:

Arkansas, Texas, Louisiana (except the parishes of St. Bernard, Plaquemines, Jefferson, St. John, St. Charles, St. James, Ascension, Assumption, Terrebonne, Lafourche, St. Mary, St. Martin, and Orleans, including the city of New Orleans), Mississippi, Alabama, Florida, Georgia, South Carolina, North Carolina, and Virginia (except the forty-eight counties designated as West Virginia, and also the counties of Berkeley, Accomac, Northhampton, Elizabeth City, York, Princess Anne, and Norfolk, including the cities of Norfolk and Portsmouth), and which excepted parts are for the present left precisely as if this proclamation were not issued.

And by virtue of the power and for the purpose aforesaid, I do order and declare that all persons held as slaves within said designated States and parts of States are, and henceforward shall be, free; and that the Executive Government of the United States, including the military and naval authorities thereof, will recognize and maintain the freedom of said persons.

And I hereby enjoin upon the people so declared to be free to abstain from all violence, unless in necessary self-defense; and I recommend to them that, in all cases when allowed, they labor faithfully for reasonable wages.

And I further declare and make known that such persons of suitable condition will be received into the armed service of the United States to garrison forts, positions, stations, and other places, and to man vessels of all sorts in said service.

And upon this act, sincerely believed to be an act of justice, warranted by the Constitution upon military necessity, I invoke the considerate judgment of mankind and the gracious favor of Almighty God.

The Gettysburg Address

". . . a new birth of freedom; . . ."

November 19, 1863

Ten sentences. Truly, in Abraham Lincoln's words, "a little speech." But more than one hundred twenty-five years later, the president's Gettysburg Address stands as one of the most profound expressions of the democratic ideal.

The occasion was the dedication of the seventeen-acre National Soldiers' Cemetery at Gettysburg, Pennsylvania, where seven thousand Union and Confederate soldiers—"these honored dead"—were buried after the titanic struggle between the two great armies five months earlier. Gettysburg was the turning point of the Civil War. The back of the rebel cause was broken. General Robert E. Lee and his colleagues in the Confederate armies now realized they were fighting a defensive war that could not end in victory.

As he rode in the train from Washington to the battlefield and cemetery, the president tried to put into words the meaning of the struggle for liberty and Union.

He did not scrawl the speech on the back of an envelope, as legend has it; rather, he worked over it for several hours in his hotel the night before the ceremony, and edited it still as he waited to be introduced at the dedication.

A crowd of 15,000 people gathered amid the battlefield debris to hear both the major address by Senator Edward Everett of Massachusetts, the greatest orator of the day, and "a few appropriate remarks" by President Lincoln. The war was well into its third year, testing whether a nation conceived in liberty and dedicated to the proposition that all men are created equal "or any nation so conceived and so dedicated" could long endure. Everett's turned out to be his most famous address—he spoke for two hours—but the world little noted nor long remembered what he said, though he received an enthusiastic ovation. After an ode performed by the Baltimore Glee Club, Lincoln rose to the occasion. Holding his scribbled-over speech in one hand, he spoke for only a couple of minutes, so brief a time that the official photographer could not prepare his camera to take a picture until the president had finished and sat down again. Applause was slight and perfunctory.

Lincoln believed that his speech "went sour." The *Harrisburg Patriot & Union* was derisive: "We will skip over the silly remarks of the president." But Everett wrote to the president, "I should be glad if I could flatter myself that I came as near to the central idea of the occasion in two hours as you did in two minutes." Lincoln's longtime supporter, the *Chicago Tribune,* was prescient: "The dedicatory remarks of President Lincoln will live among the annals of man." (When he returned to Washington, Lincoln took to his bed with a mild case of smallpox.)

Half a dozen manuscript versions of the speech exist; Lincoln varied the wording slightly as he copied it out in longhand for friends and for charitable auctions to benefit Union veterans. The most famous is that carved on the wall of the Lincoln Memorial, in Washington, D.C.

Lincoln's Gettysburg Address

Four score and seven years ago our fathers brought forth on this continent a new nation, conceived in liberty and dedicated to the proposition that all men are created equal.

Now we are engaged in a great civil war, testing whether that nation or any nation so conceived and so dedicated can long endure. We are met on a great battlefield of that war. We have come to dedicate a portion of that field as a final resting place for those who here gave their lives that that nation might live. It is altogether fitting and proper that we should do this.

But, in a larger sense, we cannot dedicate—we cannot consecrate—we cannot hallow—this ground. The brave men, living and dead, who struggled here have consecrated it far above our poor power to add or detract. The world will little note nor long remember what we say here, but it can never forget what they did here. It is for us, the living, rather, to be dedicated here to the unfinished work which they who fought here have thus far so nobly advanced.

It is rather for us to be here dedicated to the great task remaining before us—that from these honored dead we take increased devotion to that cause for which they gave the last full measure of devotion; that we here highly resolve that these dead shall not have died in vain; that this nation, under God, shall have a new birth of freedom; and that government of the people, by the people, for the people shall not perish from the earth.

The Balfour Declaration

" . . . a national home for the Jewish people, . . . "

November 2, 1917

"**Behold,** I have given up the land before you; go in and take possession of the land which the Lord hath sworn unto your fathers, to Abraham, to Isaac, and to Jacob."—Deuteronomy 1:8

It was already the fourth year of the Great War, the First World War. Many Englishmen believed that Britain's entrenched military struggle with Germany and the other Central Powers could use additional Jewish encouragement. Turkey was one of the Central Powers. The British War Cabinet decided that Jews would be natural allies in any effort to separate Palestine from the Turkish Ottoman Empire, "the sick man of Europe." Jewish support worldwide would probably be gained through the encouragement of Zionism, whose aspiration since the late nineteenth century had been the creation of an independent Jewish state in Palestine.

The brilliant Scottish statesman Arthur James Balfour had joined British Prime Minister David Lloyd George's coalition government in 1916. Balfour was dedicated to world peace. He spoke out against the persecution of Jews, declaring that "the treatment of the race has been a disgrace to Christendom." On November 2, 1917, in a letter written on the official stationery of the British Foreign Office, Balfour—now the Minister of Foreign Affairs—informed a representative of the Zionist movement, Baron Lionel Rothschild, that His Majesty's Government viewed "with favour the establishment in Palestine of a national homeland for the Jewish people." The government would use its "best endeavours to facilitate the achievement of this object. . . ." There was only one condition of this commitment: the rights of non-Jewish communities in Palestine would have to be respected. The Balfour Declaration was thus a considered act of policy by the British War Cabinet, reinforced by moral and religious motives.

Lord Rothschild responded immediately: "I can assure you that the gratitude of ten millions of people will be yours, for the British government has opened up, by their message, a prospect of safety and comfort to large masses of people who are in need of it. I dare say, you have been informed already in many parts of Russia renewed persecution has broken out."

Arabs militantly opposed a Jewish state in their midst. After the Treaty of Versailles (1919), British Colonial Secretary Winston S. Churchill preserved but refined the British commitment to Zionism. There was to be a Jewish homeland in Palestine, but other homelands could exist there as well. On July 24, 1922, the League of Nations incorporated the Balfour Declaration into the British Mandate on Palestine, the document under which the League assigned the territory to British administration. The struggle over its effectuation lasted throughout the three decades of British rule.

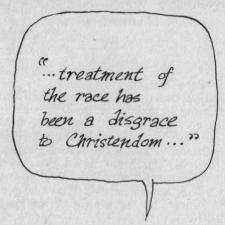

"...treatment of the race has been a disgrace to Christendom..."

(In 1925, Lord Balfour, who saw the establishment of a Jewish state as a historic act of amends, traveled to Jerusalem to deliver the opening address at the ceremony dedicating Hebrew University.)

In late 1947, the United Nations adopted a proposal to divide Palestine into a Jewish state, an Arab state, and a small internationally-administered zone including Jerusalem. The British High Commissioner for Palestine departed on May 14, 1948. Later that day, the promise of a Jewish homeland in Palestine was fulfilled at last: the state of Israel was proclaimed at Tel Aviv. Before the day was out, Arab armies from Lebanon, Syria, Jordan, Egypt, and Iraq invaded "the land of milk and honey." Israel won that war and three later wars that threatened its existence. But as the sovereign state nears its fiftieth anniversary, the envy of its twenty-one Arab neighbors, peace may be as far away as ever.

The Balfour Declaration

Foreign Office,
November 2nd, 1917.

Dear Lord Rothschild,

I have much pleasure in conveying to you, on behalf of His Majesty's Government, the following declaration of sympathy with Jewish Zionist aspirations which has been submitted to, and approved by the Cabinet.

"His Majesty's Government view with favour the establishment in Palestine of a national home for the Jewish people, and will use their best endeavours to facilitate the achievement of this object, it being clearly understood that nothing shall be done which may prejudice the civil and religious rights of existing non-Jewish communities in Palestine, or the rights and political status enjoyed by Jews in any other country."

I should be grateful if you would bring this declaration to the knowledge of the Zionist Federation.

The Treaty of Versailles

" . . . to achieve international peace and security . . . "

June 28, 1919

"Peace is only war pursued by other means."

So growled "the Tiger," the vengeful French Premier Georges Clemenceau, one of the Allied and Associated Powers' "Big Four" leaders who designed the treaty ending the First World War to prevent once-powerful, aspiring Germany from posing a military threat to Europe again.

Since the turn of the century, imperialistic, territorial, and economic rivalries had been intensifying throughout Europe. The spirit of resurgent nationalism was rampant. Violent tensions coursed through Archduke Francis Ferdinand's Central European Austro-Hungarian monarchy—which consisted of the present-day countries of Austria, Hungary, and Czechoslovakia, and parts of Italy, Poland, Romania, and Yugoslavia. The continent was a powder keg.

On June 28, 1914, Ferdinand was shot to death in Sarajevo by a teenage Serbian nationalist. Exactly one month later, desperate diplomatic manuevers ended in failed brinkmanship, what the historian A. J. P. Taylor called "war by time-table." Networks of military alliances—the Central Powers (the empires of Austria-Hungary and Germany, Bulgaria, and Turkey, which was rotting internally) and the Allied and Associated Powers (Britain, an island country with an overseas empire embracing nearly twenty-five percent of the planet's land surface; France, greedy, wracked by revanchism toward Germany, and awash with corruption; Russia, suffering terminal decay; and Italy)—made war inevitable. Japan and the United States joined the Allies later.

America's entry into the war, on April 6, 1917, carried the promise of a better ending than carnage and revenge. Eager to make the world safe for democracy, President Woodrow Wilson dubbed the conflict "the war to end all wars." The war turned out to be the most widespread and bloodiest catastrophe ever seen: by Armistice Day, more than 10 million people were dead and another 20 million were injured. No Allied soldier ever set foot in Germany, but the exhausted and all-but-starving Central Powers surrendered on November 11, 1918. The president hoped to persuade the victorious Allies to renounce territorial ambitions and to forge a new framework to safeguard world peace.

The Peace Conference dragged on for five months. The "Carthaginians," Clemenceau and British Prime Minister David Lloyd George, wore down Wilson's idealistic fourteen-point framework for the postwar era. Their countries had suffered terribly, and they were determined to exact vengeance—crushing, punishing, severe to a high degree. The 200-page treaty laid the full blame for the war on ambitious Germany. Germany was stripped of industries and raw materials.

Germany must pay for "damage of all property wherever situated belonging to any of the Allied or Associated States or their nations, . . . " Germany must reduce its military drastically. Germany must surrender its colonies in China, the Pacific, and Africa. Germany must return Alsace-Lorraine to France, the "imperial land" that had been pried away by Germany's "Iron Chancellor," Otto von Bismarck, in 1870. Germany must turn over for French operation the coal mines in the rich industrial Saar Valley. Thus, Germany lost 13 percent of its prewar territory, 10 percent of its population, 75 percent of its iron ore, and 25 percent of its best coal; it was also required to pay the victorious countries about $33 billion in reparations in forty-two annual payments. The treaty redrew the map of Europe, creating nine new sovereign states—the three Baltic countries of Estonia, Latvia, and Lithuania, Yugoslavia, Czechoslovakia, Poland (with a sea corridor separating East Prussia from Germany), Finland, Hungary, and Austria—and enlarging Romania and Italy at the expense of Russia and Austria.

President Wilson's Fourteen Points, which Germany thought would be the basis for the treaty, included a provision for "a general association of nations . . . " Still smarting from the concessions he had been forced to make, Wilson clung to the League as the sole justification for the treaty, which included a Covenant for a new world organization, the League of Nations. Despite a determined campaign by Wilson which destroyed his health, the Senate ratified neither the treaty nor the Covenant. Republican negativism and isolationism ruled the day. (On July 2, 1921, Washington merely declared its war with Germany was over.)

The bitterness that prevailed in Germany and Austria over the treaty and the war—Berlin denounced the treaty as a document of hatred and delusion, "a peace of violence"—sowed the seeds of a second, far more catastrophic war twenty years after the Treaty of Versailles was signed in the splendor of the Chateau of Versailles's Great Hall of Mirrors, on June 28, 1919, the fifth anniversary of the assassination of Archduke Francis Ferdinand.

Versailles Peace Treaty

The Covenant of the League of Nations

The High Contracting Parties,

In order to promote international cooperation and to achieve international peace and security

by the acceptance of obligations not to resort to war,

by the prescription of open, just and honourable relations between nations,

by the firm establishment of the understandings of international law as the actual rule of conduct among Governments, and

by the maintenance of justice and a scrupulous respect for all treaty obligations in the dealings of organized peoples with one another,

Agree to this Covenant of the League of Nations.

Article 1. The original Members of the League of Nations shall be those of the Signatories which are named in the Annex to this Covenant and also such of those other States named in the Annex as shall accede without reservation to this Covenant.

Article 2. The action of the League under this Covenant shall be effected through the instrumentality of an Assembly and of a Council, with a permanent Secretariat.

Article 3. The Assembly shall consist of Representatives of the Members of the League.

Article 4. The Council may deal at its meetings with any matter within the sphere of action of the League or affecting the peace of the world.

Article 8. The Members of the League recognize that the maintenance of peace requires the reduction of national armaments to the lowest point consistent with national safety and the enforcement by common action of international obligations. . . .

Article 11. Any war or threat of war, whether immediately affecting any of the Members of the League or not, is hereby declared a matter of concern to the whole League, and the League shall take any action that may be deemed wise and effectual to safeguard the peace of nations. In case any such emergency should arise the Secretary-General shall on the request of any Member of the League forthwith summon a meeting of the Council.

It is also declared to be the friendly right of each Member of the League to bring to the attention of the Assembly or of the Council any circumstance whatever affecting international relations which threat-

ens to disturb international peace or the good understanding between nations upon which peace depends.

Article 12. The Members of the League agree that if there should arise between them any dispute likely to lead to a rupture, they will submit the matter either to arbitration or to inquiry by the Council, and they agree in no case to resort to war until three months after the award by the arbitrators or the report by the Council.

Article 13. The Members of the League agree that whenever any dispute shall arise between them which they recognize to be suitable for submission to arbitration and which cannot be satisfactorily settled by diplomacy, they will submit the whole subject-matter to arbitration.

The Members of the League agree that they will carry out in full good faith any award that may be rendered, and that they will not resort to war against a Member of the League which complies therewith. In the event of any failure to carry out such an award, the Council shall propose what steps should be taken to give effect thereto.

Article 14. The Council shall formulate and submit to the Members of the League for adoption plans for the establishment of a Permanent Court of International Justice. The Court shall be competent to hear and determine any dispute of an international character which the parties thereto submit to it. The Court may also give an advisory opinion upon any dispute or question referred to it by the Council or by the Assembly. . . .

Article 16. Should any Member of the League resort to war in disregard of its covenants . . . , it shall *ipso facto* be deemed to have committed an act of war against all other Members of the League, which hereby undertake immediately to subject it to the severance of all trade or financial relations, the prohibition of all intercourse between their nationals and the nationals of the covenant-breaking State, and the prevention of all financial, commercial or personal intercourse between the nationals of the covenant-breaking State and the nationals of any other State, whether a Member of the League or not.

It shall be the duty of the Council in such case to recommend to the several Governments concerned what effective military, naval or air force the Members of the League shall severally contribute to the armed forces to be used to protect the covenants of the League.

The Members of the League agree, further, that they will mutually support one another in the financial and economic measures which are taken under this Article, in order to minimize the loss and inconvenience resulting from the above measures, and that they will mutually support one another in resisting any special measures aimed at one of their number by the covenant-breaking State, and that they will take the necessary steps to afford passage through their territory to the forces of any of the Members of the League which are cooperating to protect the covenants of the League. . . .

Article 21. Nothing in this Covenant shall be deemed to affect the validity of international engagements, such as treaties of arbitration or regional understandings like the Monroe Doctrine, for securing the maintenance of peace.

Article 22. To those colonies and territories which as a consequence of the late war have ceased to be under the sovereignty of the States which formerly governed them and which are inhabited by peoples not yet able to stand by themselves under the strenuous conditions of the modern world, there should be applied the principle that the well-being and development of such peoples form a sacred trust of civilization and that securities for the performance of this trust should be embodied in this Covenant.

The best method of giving practical effect to this principle is that the tutelage of such peoples should be entrusted to advanced nations who by reason of their resources, their experience or their geographical position can best undertake this responsibility, and who are willing to accept it, and that this tutelage should be exercised by them as Mandatories on behalf of the League.

The character of the mandate must differ according to the stage of the development of the people, the geographical situation of the territory, its economic conditions and other similar circumstances.

Certain communities formerly belonging to the Turkish Empire have reached a stage of development where their existence as independent nations can be provisionally recognized subject to the rendering of administrative advice and assistance by a Mandatory until such time as they are able to stand alone. The wishes of these communities must be a principal consideration in the selection of the Mandatory.

Other peoples, especially those of Central Africa, are at such a stage that the Mandatory must be responsible for the administration of the territory under conditions which will guarantee freedom of conscience and religion, subject only to the maintenance of public order and morals; the prohibition of abuses such as the slave trade, the arms traffic and the liquor traffic, and the prevention of the establishment of fortifications or military and naval bases and of military training of the natives for other than police purposes and the defence of territory, and will also secure equal opportunities for the trade and commerce of other Members of the League.

There are territories, such as Southwest Africa and certain of the South Pacific Islands, which, owing to the sparseness of their population, or their small size, or their remoteness from the centres of civilization, or their geographical contiguity to the territory of the Mandatory, and other circumstances, can be best administered under the laws of the Mandatory as integral portions of its territory, subject to the safeguards above mentioned in the interests of the indigenous population.

Article 23. Subject to and in accordance with the provisions of international conventions existing or hereafter to be agreed upon, the Members of the League:

(a) will endeavour to secure and maintain fair and humane conditions of labour for men, women, and children, both in their own countries and in all countries to which their commercial and industrial relations extend, and for that purpose will establish and maintain the necessary international organizations;

(b) undertake to secure just treatment of the native inhabitants of territories under their control;

(c) will entrust the League with the general supervision over the execution of agreements with regard to the traffic in women and children, and the traffic in opium and other dangerous drugs;

(d) will entrust the League with the general supervision of the trade in arms and ammunition with the countries in which the control of this traffic is necessary in the common interest;

(e) will make provision to secure and maintain freedom of communications and of transit and equitable treatment for the commerce of all Members of the League. In this connection, the special necessities of the regions devastated during the war of 1914–1918 shall be borne in mind;

(f) will endeavour to take steps in matters of international concern for the prevention and control of disease.

The Charter
of the United Nations

" . . . to . . . live together in peace . . . "

October 24, 1945

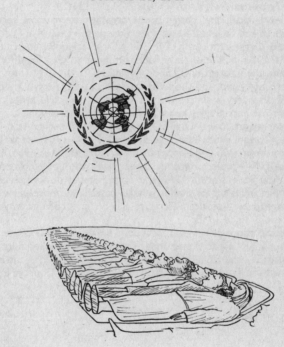

In 1942, twenty-six countries at war with the Axis powers (principally with Germany, Italy, and Japan) pledged to continue their efforts jointly and not to make peace separately. United States President Franklin D. Roosevelt coined the corporate name United Nations.* On October 20, 1943, an official declaration for an international organization—the United Nations—to replace the moribund League of Nations was proposed in the Moscow Declaration adopted by China, Great Britain, the U.S., and the Union of Soviet Socialist Republics.

*Millions of tongues record thee, and anew
Their children's lips shall echo them, and say—
"Here, where the sword united nations drew,
Our countrymen were warring on that day!"
And this is much, and all which will not pass away.
—Lord Byron

The Charter of the United Nations was adopted at the founding conference of the U.N., April 25–June 26, 1945, in San Francisco, and ratified on October 24, which is celebrated today as United Nations Day. The United Nations would "save succeeding generations from the scourge of war, . . . reaffirm faith in fundamental human rights, . . . promote social programs and better standards of life in larger freedom."

Fifty-one allied sovereign states and nations, including two constituent republics of the Soviet Union, joined the U.N. immediately. Membership tripled to 159 in the next thirty years. On March 10, 1992, membership stood at 175, with Russia taking over the seat of the late U.S.S.R. (The only prominent non-member country is perpetually neutral Switzerland.)

Specialized agencies and commissions provide international services in economic, cultural, and technical fields. They include the Universal Postal Union, the World Health Organization, the U.N. Educational, Scientific, and Cultural Organization, the International Monetary Fund, the International Fund for Agricultural Development, the International Labor Organization, the U.N. International Children's Emergency Fund, and the World Intellectual Property Organization.

The U.N. also serves as the world's organ of collective security, promoting disarmament and encouraging peaceful solutions to international disputes. Its first military observer group was UNTSO, created in 1948 during Arab-Israeli hostilities. In the Korean War, "the coldest war" (1950–1953), peak U.N. military strength was about 400,000—most of them Americans. In 1956, U.S. pressure through the U.N.—after an atomic threat from the Soviet Union—brought a ceasefire in the Suez War. In 1962, the United States worked through the U.N. to force the dismantling of Soviet missile bases in Cuba capable of launching nuclear warheads at American territory. There have been twenty-three peacekeeping missions since 1948.

The United Nations places no restrictions on the eligibility of men and women to participate in any capacity and under conditions of equality in its principal and subsidiary organs—the General Assembly, the Security Council, the Economic and Social Council, the Trusteeship Council, the International Court of Justice, and the Secretariat.

Preamble of the Charter
of the United Nations

WE THE PEOPLES OF THE UNITED NATIONS
DETERMINED

to save succeeding generations from the scourge of war, which twice in our lifetime has brought untold sorrow to mankind, and

to reaffirm faith in fundamental human rights, in the dignity and worth of the human person, in the equal rights of men and women and of nations large and small, and

to establish conditions under which justice and respect for the obligations arising from treaties and other sources of international law can be maintained, and

to promote social progress and better standards of life in larger freedom,

AND FOR THESE ENDS

to practice tolerance and live together in peace with one another as good neighbours, and

to unite our strength to maintain international peace and security, and

to ensure, by the acceptance of principles and the institution of methods, that armed force shall not be used, save in the common interest, and

to employ international machinery for the promotion of the economic and social advancement of all peoples,

HAVE RESOLVED TO COMBINE OUR EFFORTS TO ACCOMPLISH THESE AIMS.

Accordingly, our respective Governments, through representatives assembled in the city of San Francisco, who have exhibited their full powers found to be in good and due form, have agreed to the present Charter of the United Nations and do hereby establish an international organization to be known as the United Nations.

The Universal Declaration of Human Rights

" . . . born free and equal in dignity and rights."

December 10, 1948

Without a dissenting vote, the 56-member General Assembly of the United Nations, meeting in Paris, adopted the Universal Declaration of Human Rights three years after the ratification of the Charter of the United Nations. It was the first time that an organized international community of countries had promulgated a declaration of human rights and fundamental freedoms. Eight members abstained from voting: the Soviet Union and the two member constituent republics, Byelorussia and Ukraine; Czechoslovakia; Poland; Saudi Arabia; South Africa; and Yugoslavia.

In 1988, Secretary General Javier Perez de Cuellar hailed the document on its fortieth anniversary as "a major milestone in human progress, bringing realization to the [U.N.] Charter principle that universal respect for human rights is the common concern of all governments and all people . . . serving in its field as the conscience for the world and a standard against which the attitudes of societies and governments can be measured." Objectives and principles in the Declaration find reflection today in the constitutions and laws of many countries.

It was at the founding conference of the world body in San Francisco in the spring of 1945 that proposals for a declaration of human rights were made by Panama, Mexico, and Cuba. The chairman of the Human Rights Commission responsible for preparing the document was U.S. delegate Eleanor Roosevelt, the widow of President Franklin D. Roosevelt, whose dream it had been to organize the United Nations to preserve world peace. Reviews and revisions occupied more than eighty meetings of the commission over three years. Virtually all basic problems of human life were discussed, from God and the State to children and social security. Mrs. Roosevelt called it "a good document, though not perfect."* The president of the General Assembly announced that Mrs. Roosevelt's work had "raised a great name to an even greater honor."

Since 1948, many international instruments have been adopted to protect specific rights. These include: the 1959 Declaration of the Rights of the Child; the 1961 Convention on the Reduction of Statelessness; the 1963 U.N. Declaration on the Elimination of All Forms of Racial Discrimination; the 1966 Protocol Relating to the Status of Refugees; the 1971 Declaration on the Rights of Mentally Retarded Persons; the 1974 Universal Declaration on the Eradication of Hunger

*Some elements that were not accepted: "Man is a citizen both of his State and of the world. . . . Everyone has the right, either individually or in association with others, to petition the government of his State or the United Nations for redress of grievance . . . "

and Malnutrition; the 1975 Declaration on the Rights of Disabled Persons; and the 1979 Convention on the Elimination of All Forms of Discrimination against Women.

In the early 1990s, the world's poorest countries were generally also the least free. An independent U.N. agency classified Sweden as the world's freest country and Iraq as the least free. The United States ranked thirteenth. Only a quarter of the world's population of 5.3 billion live in totally free countries. The agency also ranked nations on a human-need index measuring education, life expectancy, and economic wealth. Japan, which has four times as many teachers as soldiers, ranks at the top; the United States is seventh; the oil-producing Arab countries rank poorly because they neglect the education of girls. The poorest African states occupy the bottom rungs.

The Universal Declaration of Human Rights

Whereas recognition of the inherent dignity and of the equal and inalienable rights of all members of the human family is the foundation of freedom, justice and peace in the world,

Whereas disregard and contempt for human rights have resulted in barbarous acts which have outraged the conscience of mankind, and the advent of a world in which human beings shall enjoy freedom of speech and belief and freedom from fear and want has been proclaimed as the highest aspiration of the common people,

Whereas it is essential, if man is not to be compelled to have recourse, as a last resort, to rebellion against tyranny and oppression, that human rights should be protected by the rule of law,

Whereas it is essential to promote the development of friendly relations between nations,

Whereas the peoples of the United Nations have in the Charter reaffirmed their faith in fundamental human rights, in the dignity and worth of the human person and in the equal rights of men and women and have determined to promote social progress and better standards of life in larger freedom,

Whereas Member States have pledged themselves to achieve, in cooperation with the United Nations, the promotion of universal respect for and observance of human rights and fundamental freedoms,

Whereas a common understanding of these rights and freedoms is of the greatest importance for the full realization of this pledge,

Now, Therefore,

THE GENERAL ASSEMBLY
proclaims

Article 1. All human beings are born free and equal in dignity and rights. They are endowed with reason and conscience and should act towards one another in a spirit of brotherhood.

Article 2. Everyone is entitled to all the rights and freedoms set forth in this Declaration, without distinction of any kind, such as race, colour, sex, language, religion, political or other opinion, national or social origin, property, birth or other status.

Article 3. Everyone has the right to life, liberty and security of person.

Article 4. No one shall be held in slavery or servitude; slavery and the slave trade shall be prohibited in all their forms.

Article 5. No one shall be subjected to torture or to cruel, inhuman or degrading treatment or punishment.

Article 6. Everyone has the right to recognition everywhere as a person before the law.

Article 7. All are equal before the law and are entitled without any discrimination to equal protection of the law. All are entitled to equal protection against any discrimination in violation of this Declaration and against any incitement to such discrimination.

Article 8. Everyone has the right to an effective remedy by the competent national tribunals for acts violating the fundamental rights granted him by the constitution or by law.

Article 9. No one shall be subjected to arbitrary arrest, detention or exile.

Article 10. Everyone is entitled in full equality to a fair and public hearing by an independent and impartial tribunal, in the determination of his rights and obligations and of any criminal charge against him.

Article 11. (1) Everyone charged with a penal offence has the right to be presumed innocent until proved guilty according to law in a public trial at which he has had all the guarantees necessary for his defence. . . .

Article 13. (1) Everyone has the right to freedom of movement and residence within the borders of each state.
(2) Everyone has the right to leave any country, including his own, and to return to his country.

Article 14. (1) Everyone has the right to seek and to enjoy in other countries asylum from persecution. . . .

Article 15.
. . . (2) No one shall be arbitrarily deprived of his nationality nor denied the right to change his nationality.

Article 16. (1) Men and women of full age, without any limitation due to race, nationality or religion, have the right to marry and to found a family. They are entitled to equal rights as to marriage, during marriage and at its dissolution. . . .
(3) The family is the natural and fundamental group unit of society and is entitled to protection by society and the State.

Article 17. (1) Everyone has the right to own property alone as well as in association with others.
(2) No one shall be arbitrarily deprived of his property.

Article 18. Everyone has the right to freedom of thought, conscience and religion; this right includes freedom to change his religion or belief, and freedom, either alone or in community with others and in public or private, to manifest his religion or belief in teaching, practice, worship and observance.

Article 19. Everyone has the right to freedom of opinion and expression; this right includes freedom to hold opinions without interference and to

seek, receive and impart information and ideas through any media and regardless of frontiers.

Article 20. (1) Everyone has the right to freedom of peaceful assembly and association. . . .

Article 21. (1) Everyone has the right to take part in the government of his country, directly or through freely chosen representatives. . . .

(3) The will of the people shall be the basis of the authority of government; this will shall be expressed in periodic and genuine elections which shall be by universal and equal suffrage and shall be held by secret vote or by equivalent free voting procedures.

Article 22. Everyone, as a member of society, has the right to social security and is entitled to realization, through national effort and international co-operation and in accordance with the organization and resources of each State, of the economic, social and cultural rights indispensable for his dignity and the free development of his personality.

Article 23. (1) Everyone has the right to work, to free choice of employment, to just and favourable conditions of work and to protection against unemployment.
(2) Everyone, without any discrimination, has the right to equal pay for equal work.

Article 24. Everyone has the right to rest and leisure, including reasonable limitation of working hours and periodic holidays with pay.

Article 25. (1) Everyone has the right to a standard of living adequate for the health and well-being of himself and of his family, including food, clothing, housing and medical care and necessary social services, and the right to security in the event of unemployment, sickness, disability, widowhood, old age or other lack of livelihood in circumstances beyond his control.
(2) Motherhood and childhood are entitled to special care and assistance. All children, whether born in or out of wedlock, shall enjoy the same social protection.

Article 26. (1) Everyone has the right to education. Education shall be free, at least in the elementary and fundamental stages. . . .
(2) Education shall be directed to the full development of the human personality and to the strengthening of respect for human rights and fundamental freedoms. . . .
(3) Parents have a prior right to choose the kind of education that shall be given to their children.

Article 27.
. . . (2) Everyone has the right to the protection of the moral and material interests resulting from any scientific, literary or artistic production of which he is the author.

Article 29. (1) Everyone has duties to the community in which alone the free and full development of his personality is possible. . . .

The Civil Rights Acts of 1964 and 1968 and the Voting Rights Act of 1965

"All persons shall be entitled . . . No voting qualification . . . shall be imposed or applied . . . "

July 2, 1964; April 11, 1968; August 6, 1965

Even after the end of the Civil War and the abolition of slavery by the Thirteenth Amendment to the Constitution, the problems of the freed slaves confronted the United States still. From Appomattox and Reconstruction to the present, the quest to eradicate the stain of slavery from American history has not been fulfilled.

In 1866, Congress enacted the first Civil Rights Act. It was designed to recognize four million or so people—freed slaves and free African-Americans—as citizens on an equal basis with whites. Challenges to its constitutionality forced Congress to write much of the Act's most important language into the Fourteenth Amendment, ratified in 1868, which forbids any state to deny "to any person within its jurisdiction the equal protection of the laws." In 1870, during President Ulysses S. Grant's first term, the Fifteenth Amendment (and third "Civil War amendment") declared that the right to vote "shall not be denied . . . on account of race, color, or previous condition of servitude." Congress enacted legislation to enforce it. Laws turned out to be of little value because of congressional inattention, executive inaction, and judicial indifference. Some civil rights laws were struck down in the early 1880s as unconstitutional.

Not until 1957 did Congress, under the leadership of a vigorous southerner, Senator Lyndon B. Johnson, attempt to adopt another Civil Rights Act. The measure provided some (but not enough) protection for African-Americans who wanted to vote; it also established the Civil Rights Commission. Johnson also championed the 1960 Civil Rights Act, which strengthened the 1957 measure.

The civil rights movement shamed most white Americans, including the administration of President John F. Kennedy, into exploring the possibility of serious action to vindicate African-Americans' civil rights. Kennedy made a new civil rights bill a high priority. In his first address to Congress following the assassination of Kennedy, President Johnson (the former senator) repeatedly invoked the murdered president's name and urged that the bill be passed as a memorial to him: "Let this session of Congress be known as the session [that] did more for civil rights than the last hundred sessions combined." Using his remarkable legislative and political skills during the Herculean struggle, Johnson mustered the support of liberals such as Senator Hubert H. Humphrey and conservatives such as Senator

Everett M. Dirksen, and broke a three-month filibuster led by southern senators—a feat that was without precedent. The president said that "our mission is at once the oldest and the most basic of this country: to right wrong, to do justice, to serve men," and he asked the country to "close the springs of racial poison" and for peaceful compliance: "It is not just Negroes, but really it is all of us who must overcome the crippling legacy of bigotry and injustice."

Signed on July 2, 1964, by the first southern chief executive since Andrew Johnson, the Civil Rights Act of 1964 was the most sweeping civil rights measure since Reconstruction. It prohibited discrimination in places of public accommodation (including hotels, motels, restaurants, and places of amusement); authorized the attorney general to bring suits to desegregate schools; established an Equal Opportunity Commission to combat job discrimination; and gave federal agencies the authority to withhold federal funds from state-run programs that discriminated on the basis of race.

On August 6 the next year, the Voting Rights Act provided for effective federal protection enabling blacks to register and vote. President Johnson called it a "triumph as huge as any victory that has ever been won on any battlefield . . . ," adding that the act was "a great challenge" to black leadership, which must teach blacks their responsibilities and lead them to exercise their rights.

On April 11, 1968, two days after the funeral of the assassinated civil rights leader and Nobel Peace Prize winner Martin Luther King, Jr., Congress passed an act prohibiting discrimination on the basis of race, religion, or national origin in selling or renting houses. The legislation affected about 80 percent of the country's housing. It was a major victory for civil rights groups.

President Johnson described the "civil rights problem" as "the most difficult domestic issue we have ever faced." The more it was grappled with, "the more we realize that the position of minorities in American society is defined not merely by law, but by social, educational, and economic conditions." An "ideal America" would not need to seek new laws guaranteeing the rights of citizens.

In January 1992, the United States Supreme Court limited the scope of the 1965 Voting Rights Act, retreating from its often-stated view that the act "should be given the broadest possible scope." The Court ruled that the reorganization of two county boards in Alabama was not covered by the act, which prohibits most southern states and some parts of northern states from adopting any new "practice or procedure with respect to voting" without first getting approval from the attorney general or the Federal District Court. The Court rejected arguments that the Bush administration had put forward on behalf of black elected officials. The reorganizations were supported by the white incumbents.

The Civil Rights Act of 1964

TITLE I
VOTING RIGHTS

Sec. 101 (2). No person acting under color of law shall—

(A) in determining whether any individual is qualified under State law or laws to vote in any Federal election, apply any standard, practice, or procedure different from the standards, practices, or procedures applied under such law or laws to other individuals within the same county, parish, or similar political subdivision who have been found by State officials to be qualified to vote; . . .

TITLE II
INJUNCTIVE RELIEF AGAINST DISCRIMINATION IN PLACES OF PUBLIC ACCOMMODATION

SEC. 201. (a) All persons shall be entitled to the full and equal enjoyment of the goods, services, facilities, privileges, advantages, and accommodations of any phase of public accommodation if as defined in this section, without discrimination or segregation on the ground of race, color, religion, or national origin.

(b) Each of the following establishments which serves the public is a place of public accommodation within the meaning of this title if its operations affect commerce, or if discrimination or segregation by it is supported by State action:

(1) any inn, motel, or other establishment which provides lodging to transient guests, other than an establishment located within a building which contains not more than five rooms for rent or hire and which is actually occupied by the proprietor of such establishment as his residence;

(2) any restaurant, cafeteria, lunch room, lunch counter, soda fountain, or other facility principally engaged in selling food for consumption on the premises . . .

(3) any motion picture house, theater, concert hall, sports arena, stadium or other place of exhibition or entertainment. . . .

SEC. 202. All persons shall be entitled to be free, at any establishment or place, from discrimination or segregation of any kind on the ground of race, color, religion, or national origin, if such discrimination or segregation is or purports to be required by any law, statute, ordinance, regulation, rule, or order of a State or any agency or political subdivision thereof. . . .

The Civil Rights Act of 1968

Sec. 2101. *Riots.*

(a) (1) Whoever travels in interstate or foreign commerce or uses any facility of interstate or foreign commerce, including, but not limited to, the mail, telegraph, telephone, radio, or television, with intent—

(A) to incite a riot; or

(B) to organize, promote, encourage, participate in, or carry on a riot; or

(C) to commit any act of violence in furtherance of a riot; or

(D) to aid or abet any person in inciting or participating in or carrying on a riot or committing any act of violence in furtherance of a riot; and who either during the course of any such travel or use or thereafter performs or attempts to perform any other overt act for any purpose specified [above]—

Shall be fined not more than $10,000, or imprisoned not more than five years, or both.

(b) As used in this chapter, the term "to incite a riot," or "to organize, promote, encourage, participate in, or carry on a riot," includes, but is not limited to, urging or instigating other persons to riot, but shall not be deemed to mean the mere oral or written (1) advocacy of ideas or (2) expression of belief, not involving advocacy of any act or acts of violence or assertion of the rightness of, or the right to commit, any such act or acts.

TITLE X
Civil Obedience
CIVIL DISORDERS

(a) (1) Whoever teaches or demonstrates to any other person the use, application, or making of any firearm or explosive or incendiary device, or technique capable of causing injury or death to persons, knowing or having reason to know or intending that the same will be unlawfully employed for use in, or in furtherance of, a civil disorder which may in any way or degree obstruct, delay, or adversely affect commerce or the movement of any article or commodity in commerce or the conduct or performance of any federally protected function; or

(2) Whoever transports or manufactures for transportation in commerce any firearm, or explosive or incendiary device, knowing or having reason to know or intending that the same will be used unlawfully in furtherance of a civil disorder; or

(3) Whoever commits or attempts to commit any act to obstruct, impede, or interfere with any fireman or law enforcement officer lawfully engaged in the lawful performance of his official duties incident to and during the commission of a civil disorder which in any way or degree obstructs, delays, or adversely affects commerce or the movement of any article or commodity in commerce or the conduct or performance of any federally protected function—

Voting Rights Act of 1965

Sec. 2. No voting qualification or prerequisite to voting, or standard, practice, or procedure shall be imposed or applied by any State or political subdivision to deny or abridge the right of any citizen of the United States to vote on account of race or color.

Sec. 3. (a) Whenever the Attorney General institutes a proceeding under any statute to enforce the guarantees of the fifteenth amendment in any State or political subdivision the court shall authorize the appointment of Federal examiners by the United States Civil Service Commission in accordance with section 6 to serve for such period of time and for such political subdivisions as court shall determine is appropriate to enforce the guarantees of the fifteenth amendment (1) as part of any interlocutory order if the court determines that the appointment of such examiners is necessary to enforce such guarantees or (2) as part of any final judgment if the court finds that violations of the fifteenth amendment justifying equitable relief have occurred in such State or subdivision: *Provided,* That the court need not authorize the appointment of examiners if any incidents of denial or abridgement of the right to vote on account of race or color (1) have been few in number and have been promptly and effectively corrected by State or local action, (2) the continuing effect of such incidents has been eliminated, and (3) there is no reasonable probability of their recurrence in the future.

SEC. 4. (a) To assure that the right of citizens of the United States to vote is not denied or abridged on account of race or color, no citizen shall be denied the right to vote in any Federal, State, or local election because of his failure to comply with any test or device in any State. . . .

(c) The phrase "test or device" shall mean any requirement that a person as a prerequisite for voting or registration for voting (1) demonstrate the ability to read, write, understand, or interpret any matter, (2) demonstrate any educational achievement or his knowledge of any particular subject, (3) possess good moral character, or (4) prove his qualifications by the voucher of registered voters or members of any other class. . . .

(e) (1) Congress hereby declares that to secure the rights under the fourteenth amendment of persons educated in American-flag schools in which the predominant classroom language was other than English, it is necessary to prohibit the States from conditioning the right to vote of such persons on ability to read, write, understand, or interpret any matter in the English language.

(2) No person who demonstrates that he has successfully completed the sixth primary grade in a public school in, or a private school accredited by, any State or territory, the District of Columbia, or the Commonwealth of Puerto Rico in which the predominant classroom language was other than English, shall be denied the right to vote in any Federal, State, or local election because of his inability to read, write, understand, or interpret any matter in the English language. . . .

ABOUT THE AUTHORS

MORT GERBERG is a writer and cartoonist who lives in New York City. He is most widely known for his panel cartoons, which appear regularly in *Publishers Weekly, The New Yorker,* and *Playboy.* He has drawn several nationally-syndicated newspaper comic strips, and has written and/or illustrated thirty books of humor for adults and children. He teaches cartooning courses and lectures. His *Cartooning: The Art and the Business* is the leading reference work in the field. Among his current books are *Geographunny,* a book of global riddles, and *Joy in Mudville: The Big Book of Baseball Humor* (with Dick Schaap).

JEROME AGEL has written and/or produced more than forty books, including collaborations with Carl Sagan, Marshall McLuhan, Buckminster Fuller, Herman Kahn, Stanley Kubrick, and Isaac Asimov. His current works include *Why in the World* (with George J. Demko), *Where on Earth?, Dr. Grammar's Writes from Wrongs, 100 Amazing Americans, Cleopatra's Nose . . . ,* and *Amending America: How the American People Have Reshaped the Constitution to Meet Their Changing Needs* (with Richard B. Bernstein, whose reading made this a better book). Mr. Gerberg and Mr. Agel's *The U.S. Constitution for Everyone* (Perigee) is in its fifteenth printing.